Pranksters Forever

An Enemies to Lovers Romance Short Story

Forever #5

S. M. Bikanu

Blurb

When a matrimony site matches me with my nemesis…

This morning when I wake up to a notification on my phone: I have a notification, from the matrimony app.

That's a first in three days since I have been on the matrimony app.

A new match has come in; someone named Abhimanyu Singh has requested my profile to be viewed. Abhimanyu Singh happens to be my nemesis since college. I feel a bitter taste in my mouth.

The app says we are a perfect match, there has to be a glitch, because Abhimanyu Singh and I never had anything in common, and there is no way we would be a match. I doubt the algorithms already.

But I'm still tempted to talk to him. After all, the man was hot.

Pranksters Forever is a light-hearted, sweet, and witty romance short story. This fun romance story has promised a happy ending. There are some cozy moments but nothing explicit.

Contents

Pranksters Forever 1

Blurb 4

Contents 6

Chapter 1 – Mismatched (Inara's POV) 7

Chapter 2 – Perfect score (Abhumanyu's POV)....................24

Chapter 3 – The date, awkward! 36

Chapter 4 – The Revelation (Inara's POV) 53

Chapter 5 – The L-word (Inara's POV) 64

About S. M. Bikanu...74

Chapter 1 – Mismatched

(Inara's POV)

I have just registered my profile with shaadi.com and Tinder. Yep, I'm playing with extremes from holy matrimony to sinful one-night stands, I want to keep my options open.

Why so desperate, you ask?

Because I have been made to realize that I have gotten old.

Like, really old.

In my head, I'm still the 21-year-old girl who left my parents' house to lead an independent life. Five years later, my mom says that I'm too old now. She also says that if I don't hurry, I might not find a good match, and I might end up a spinster. She says many more things, but I will not bore you with gory details of that verbal assault.

I am twenty-six and single, a Quality Assurance Engineer in a software firm. I sit behind a tiny desk and watch the programmers work, sipping coffee and checking their work as they wrote the code. I take pride in my job, but now I just feel like I've given up everything that makes me who I am to become this frumpy, tedious woman who talks too much and probably will die alone. And that's the best-case scenario; at this point, the worst-case is pretty terrible too. So yes: I am looking for a match on a matrimony site, could I be more desperate?

Tch... Such is life.

It's so strange, isn't it? I thought that real-life mothers can never say something hurtful to their daughters; it happens only on screen. I was wrong, so wrong.

I have always known I wanted to be financially independent. No one supported me, especially my mom. But I didn't listen to her. Now that I am twenty-six and single, I apparently have nothing to show for it. It's not that I haven't tried to achieve something; I do have a decent job, I have friends, and I have a life. But I have nothing that my mom ever wanted. I mean, I know I have more than I could ever ask for. But it's not the kind of happiness that makes my mom feel good.

Apparently, getting married at the right age is the ultimate achievement in life, and the right age is not decided by you. It is dictated by society, the society that is led by women like my mom.

It's hard to explain. I'd been thinking about it on the long train ride from my parents' home this morning. I can't forget how my dad said goodbye to me with a worried look on his lined face. And my mom fussed over me, asking me how my work was going and asking me if I was thinking about marriage.

The pressure is on. And I'm desperate, shamelessly so.

Let's see if I find a match via the matrimony app or the dating app.

✳✳✳

I am desperate, alright, and I'm also highly compulsive. It should be understood that I cannot stay away from the two apps - Shaadi.com and Tinder. I constantly check for status updates, any notifications, anything at all.

I am checking my profile on the matrimony site—again.

My finger is jumping across the screen, swiping left or right. I lick my lips and rub my palms together. Why am I getting anxious? I've been doing this now for a week, and I've received several messages from people all over India. I've been surprised at how many men have messaged me, but I understand that in the matrimony site world, I am very desirable, a rare gem, for women in India don't seem to be on these websites.

This site had a compatibility test that you must take to place your profile on the site. The test asks you questions about how you feel about various aspects of your life and how you feel about the opposite sex. It asked me about whether I wanted a romantic relationship, whether I wanted a committed relationship and the like. I answered all the questions and put my profile on the site.

Let's hope for the best.

***

Things aren't going as per the plan. After spending two weeks on both apps with no success and ruling out the weirdos, I get busy with office work and forget about marriage.

Almost!

My dear mom won't let me forget, would she?

It is a fine Saturday morning. I'm still in my pajama enjoying bread toast and jam with coffee.

My phone rings—mom calling.

Argh!

She will ruin my weekend, I just know.

But I can't NOT pick up her call.

"Hey, mom!" I say unenthusiastically.

"Inara, did you do anything to find a match?" she asks without waiting for a hello.

I roll my eyes.

"So, have you heard of this website called BharatMatrimony.com? You can register there and find a good match from all over India." She doesn't have to say which "this website" she is talking about. I just let her talk, because I know if I say anything at all, the conversation will take a sharp turn, and then it will end with some proposal.

And it did.

"You know, there's a nice boy from the Ahuja family in our neighbourhood. Their son is a businessman, and he would make a great match for you. His family has a Mercedes, and…"

"I have registered with a matrimony site, mom, and I have had some interesting matches. I will let you know if I find someone promising.

I end the conversation before it even starts.

"Oh, okay. So you let me know."

She hangs up. She doesn't even ask how my week was, or if I was okay.

Fine, now I need to get back to those apps and check if I have gotten any lucky.

I've been on the site for less than a month, I need some time to gather myself. The first few days I logged in, I chatted away, and then I realized that I had to focus. I needed to be more careful.

It is like gathering data for an experiment. I am going to log in every day and make a profile for myself, explaining what I am looking for and what I have to offer, but then I realize something: I need to make my profile realistic. I don't have to disclose everything about myself to others. So I make my profile as honest as I could, but not true to life.

What was I interested in? Puzzles, especially Sudoku.

What are my hobbies? Dieting and binge eating, haha.

What are my strengths? I can get along with anyone, but I am terrible at keeping in touch.

What are my weaknesses?

The list went on and on.

I answer the questionnaire trying my best to be honest and not say anything stupid. I've done it dozens of times before and I don't even remember why I'm doing it this time. I'm certainly not in love. I'm not even sure I know what love is. Maybe I'm just curious.

Maybe I just need to get my mom off my back.

✻✻✻

This morning when I wake up to a notification on my phone: I have a notification, from the matrimony app.

That's a first.

I see a notification that a new match has come in; someone named Abhimanyu Singh has requested my profile to be viewed.

I stare at my phone in disbelief.

Abhimanyu Singh.

I feel a bitter taste in my mouth.

Don't get me wrong. I don't write people off just by looking at their names. It's just that I know of one Abhimanyu Singh from college. We were in the same class for four years, but we never interacted. I hated him.

No, scratch that.

I hate him.

Even today!

This is my first match, and his name is Abhimanyu Singh.

What are the odds?

The app says we are a perfect match, there has to be a glitch because he has been my worst enemy in the final year of engineering. I doubt the algorithms already. Abhimanyu Singh and I never had anything in common, and there is no way we would be a match.

I stare at the screen. How can it be possible?

I don't know how to react. I'm shocked; shocked at the idea that this was my first match, that it was with him, that it was even possible.

I don't know what to do. I don't know what to feel. I don't know what to think. So, I just sat there, blank, staring at my phone, with the same notification on my screen.

I could not get myself to move, so I forced myself to step out of the bed and go to the kitchen to make something to eat. I could not bear to be in the house anymore. It is suffocating me. I need to escape from this room and bury myself in other thoughts. I need fresh air, but I have only just gotten up.

How is it possible?

But wait…

It could be some other Abhimanyu Singh. I shouldn't freak out.

I'm upset, but, I am still curious. I click on the profile. A familiar face is grinning at me.

Damn!

I stared at my phone in disbelief.

Yep, it's him. He's more handsome than I remember him to be, but he is also the same Abhimanyu Singh I have avoided almost throughout my final year of college and five years of professional life. I never thought I would see his name again. I remember when we first met, in our freshman year at college. We were in the same class but never spoke to each other, and I had a huge crush on him...

But... that's not important right now.

I am matched with the biggest prankster ever...

I am matched with the guy who made my life a living hell...

I am matched with Abhimanyu Singh, my crush who I wanted to flirt with but never asked out. Are you effing kidding me?

What are the odds?

And what are the odds of running into him on a matrimony site?

It is not possible. Not possible at all.

Why do I hate him, you ask?

I always wanted to talk to him, to flirt with him, to perhaps go out with him. I always felt that he liked me back.

But he never asked me out.

Instead, he nominated us for the best couple of the year.

***

The emcee steps up onto the platform, holding a microphone.

"Here we are again at the closing ceremony of the department festival of the year. This year has been a little low-key, but we've seen some very nice ceremonies. Now, to announce the winner of the best couple award... Let's hear the nominees..."

He looks down at the cue card in his hand.

"Chetan and Komal..." the announcement is met with a cheer.

Chetan who has been anxiously sitting on their couch stands up in anticipation, and I nudge Komal who is blushing in response. Chetan grins like a proud father as he and Komal walk up to the stage. We crowd applaud and cheer with pride as the announcement is met with cheers and whistles.

"Arafat and Naheed," the emcee calls.

This couple is welcomed with moderate excitement. Perhaps, it is only a few people who favour the couple. Arafat and Naheed get up at once, smiling as they walk to the stage, surrounded by cheers. The crowd applauds enthusiastically with pride, but their cheer does not quite match that of the first couple.

"Vivek and Anya..."

This couple is greeted with a roar of approval. Vivek and Anya are on their feet, jumping up and down and clapping in anticipation of the announcement. Vivek jumps in surprise when he hears his name called out. I guess he has not been expecting any sort of acknowledgement... perhaps even a grimace, but never applause. Anya nudges him hard in the arm, they walk up to the dais and take their place on the platform.

"I think the winner is clear," I whisper to myself. Even though I have voted for Komal and Chetan, I know the last couple will win.

But the emcee has one more couple to announce because he is looking down at the cue card. He looks straight at me with a strange look in his eye.

What is going on? Why is he looking at me? Is my name up there? Who with? Oh, goodness, what is going on?

He waits for a moment, clears his throat, and moves on to the next introduction.

"Abhimanyu and Inara..."

What the eff?

"Woohoo!" This meets with the loudest cheer of tonight. People are clapping frantically.

I look at him, who seems genuinely happy. I can feel attention everyone turning to us with interest. My face goes red as I swallow my anger. I feel stupid and dizzy.

My heart is thudding crazily as he gets up and walks to me. With every step of his, my heart is sinking lower and lower. This can't be true. This can't be happening?

Abhimanyu is grinning widely as he reaches me and extends his hand. Do I really have to get up now and place my hand in Abhimanyu's?

Are you effing kidding me?

Everyone watches us expectantly.

Following pin-drop silence, I get up, pick up my purse and leave.

✳✳✳

Yeah, so now you know why I hate Abhimanyu Singh. He ruined college life for me after he played a prank during college fest. And I hate him ever since. That night of the festival changed my life for me. Ever since that night, I could never be the same confident girl that I was. If I had the option to appear only for final exams without attending classes, I would have done that.

And I am determined to never accept the match.

I will never go out with Abhimanyu Singh, no matter how good-looking he is.

I will never go out Abhimanyu Singh even if he is the hottest guy I have ever seen.

I will never go out with the guy who ruined college life for me. his trophy wife.

I will not.

It is best not to respond, I think.   I will ignore his message.

But, I am curious.

We met in our freshman year at college. We were in the same class but never spoke to each other. But I had a huge crush on him, and I wanted to talk to him, and maybe see if we could ever go out on a date. And then the college fest happened and Abhimanyu played a prank on me. Now, I think, am I blowing it out of proportion?

Today, I think that the prank was innocent enough, but at the time I was just a young and immature girl who did not know how to react to that crazy situation. After that night, I pushed myself into a inpenetrable shell. It ruined any chance of having fun during college years. I was so embarrassed and angry that I cut off all contact with him, the emcee, and everyone else in the class.

Now, here we are, matched on a dating app. I can't believe it. I have been so careful to avoid him since college, and yet he has found his way back into my life.

I should just reject him.

Hi Abhimanyu,

What a coincidence!

I don't believe in coincidences, so I'm shocked to be matched with you I am sorry that I have to un-match you, but I don't intend to ever be matched with you.

Regards,

Inara

Nah, that would give him a reason to think that he has been bothering me all these years. I can't give him the pleasure of knowing that he ruined my peace. I press backspace until the message window is empty and then start over.

I am about to delete his request but then hesitate. I have always wondered what could have happened between us if it wasn't for that silly prank. Maybe this is my chance to find out. Maybe this is my way to repay for that prank.

I take a deep breath and send him a message.

Hi Abhimanyu Singh,

It's Inara. I know it's been a while, but I thought I'd reach out. How have you been?"

Regards,

Inara

I hesitate for several minutes, my heart beating faster with every passing second. I am not sure what I am expecting, but I am hopeful. Maybe this time things would turn out differently.

I press send.

Chapter 2 – Perfect score (Abhumanyu's POV)

I walk to the mobile shop near me. I need to pick up my mobile phone. A week ago I accidentally dropped it in my balcony shattering the screen. For the past twod days it has been withtbhr mobile shop owner to fix it. It doesn't take two days to dox a broken screen..it's just that I was drowned in work and had no time to collect it.

Until today.

It's alright. I could survive without my phone because I have two phones. My work phone is always with me so I don't really miss much I don't have my personal phone. I talk to my .other every weekend and that's not due until Sunday so I am good. My personal phone is only for playing pool (I love that app) and for Tinder. I am on Tinder because I don't want an arranged marriage with a girl my mother chooses for me. I want to find a life partner not a subordinate. My mother's idea of a bride is drastically different from mine. Let's just say that I trust Tinder for bringing me a better match.

I out the phone, my personal for charging and go to take a shower. After shower and dinner I pick up my phone. It is finally time to play some pool online. I switch on the mobile. Within a minute I hear a million buzzes as notifications pop on the screen and disappear.

How many notifications are there?

Most of the notifications are from Calendar. I am a to-do list kinda guy who likes making lists and not work in them. So my calendar is full or recurring events that I never act upon. I don't even need to look at those notifications. But i should probably clear them. They are just becoming a nuisance.

Some notifications are from Gmail and some from message so I ignore them all. Many notifications are from Google Play Store and I take a mental note to look at the updates later before accepting the updates.

And the last and most interesting part... I have some notifications on Tinder. Not one, not two but several profile matches.

Huh?

That's not too bad for less than three days of being on this app. For a guy who just got on Tinder and had several matches, how do I feel?

I feel excited. It's natural for someone who has just started using a dating app and has received several matches to feel excited and possibly a little overwhelmed. It can be thrilling to know that there are people who are interested in getting to know you, and it's understandable to feel a sense of accomplishment or validation from receiving matches.

As of this moment, I feel like the king of the world. Being appreciated, being wanted, it means so much. I have always been the attention-seeker. Pranking others was one of my favourite things to get other's attention. I have been the "prankster" in every group I have been, and college was just madness. If I had a nickle for every time I pranked someone, I would be a billionaire.

But I digress. I could reminisce the past some other time. Right now, I have to look at these matches.

31 matches on Tinder

Oh, shit!

Now it hits me.

This is so overwhelming to see so many matches in there days.

Wait… What if these aren't good matches? I mean quantity doesn't necessarily mean quality, right? It's important to keep in mind that getting 31 matches on a dating app does not necessarily mean that these people are a good fit for me or that a relationship will necessarily develop. I should keep in mind that these are just algorithms, one can't rely on these algorithms for finding true love. I should probably first talk to these matches, take my time to get to know them if I like someone.

Would I like someone? I have 31 matches. I think there is a fair chance that at least one of them is not a psycho.

I walk to the corner of the living room and sit at my work desk by the window, this is where I like to sit even when I'm not working.

I let out a sigh of exasperation before opening the app. The first few are just not my type, I can tell just by their profile pictures. They were all dressed provocatively. Some photos were poorly as if they were taken in a washroom or something. The others, I reject them because their profile pictures are clicked from a non-flattering angle.

I keep scrolling through the latest batch of Tinder matches. I haven't been on the app for long so I have not gotten used to the ups and downs of online dating. I am feeling especially frustrated. Out of the 31 matches I have gotten, none seem promising a few seemed remotely promising. Most are either too young, too old, or just plain unsuitable. I sigh and swipe left on yet another profile, feeling a little bit dejected.

It's been all 31 matches.

Unbelievable!

I can't seem to find anyone decent on this app. It's like everyone's just looking for a hookup and nothing else. But then, it's Tinder. What else can I expect?

I don't give up, thought. Not yet. There are plenty of fish in the sea. I will just keep swiping until I find someone special. I am not losing hope so soon.

✻✻✻

After having my evening coffee, I pick up my phone again, this time to find something to watch before going to bed.

As I scroll through my phone, I am surprised to see a message from my mother. She has always been a bit of a matchmaker, and I know that she was always on the lookout for potential partners for me.

I open the message and see a picture of a woman I don't recognize. She is pretty, with long brown hair and big brown eyes, and she is smiling at the camera. The smile isn't seductive or alluring, it is just a genuine smile, one that is rare to find these days.

"Who's this?" I ask, tapping on the message to reply.

"That's Inara, her profile matched with yours ona matrimony site."

I can't believe it. I have always known that my mother is eager for me to get married, but I have never thought she would go so far as to create a profile for me without my consent.

Feeling a mix of anger and embarrassment, I called her. My mother is busy cooking.

"How could you do this to me, Ma?" I exclaim. "I can't believe you registered me on a matrimony app without even asking me."

My mother looks up at the phone, surprisedm almost shocked.

"What are you talking about, beta? I'm just trying to help you find a nice girl to settle down with. You're not getting any younger, you know."

I sigh. I can try to talk to her more calmly.

"I saw her pictures and I think she studied at the same college. She also lives in Pune. I thought you might be interested in meeting up with her. She's a nice girl, and I think you two would make a cute couple."

"I know that, Ma. But I have the right to choose my own partner. I don't want you to find a wife for me. I want to find love on my own terms."

Ma looks a little bit taken aback, but she nods.

"I understand, beta. I'm sorry if I overstepped my bounds. I just want what's best for you," she says.

As I look at my mother's face, I couldn't help but feel a pang of guilt. I have been so caught up in my own problems that I was rude and dismissive of her, and I know that I had hurt her feelings.

"I'm sorry, Ma," I say. I wish I was there with her, I wish I could reaching out to take her hand. "I shouldn't have been so rude to you. I know that you only want what's best for me."

Ma smiled, her eyes filling with tears.

"It's okay, beta. I understand that you're going through a tough time. I just wish you would confide in me more. I'm here for you, always."

I know, she is there for me, always.

I smile at my mother, feeling a wave of love and gratitude wash over me. I am the luckiest to have such a supportive and understanding mother, and I vow to be more considerate of her feelings in the future.

I am feeling a little bit guilty for snapping at her. I knew that she meant well, and I couldn't blame her for wanting me to be happy. But I also knew that I needed to assert my own independence and find love on my own terms.

Since I have already been rude to her, I don't want to repeat that, since I have already hurt her once, I don't want to do that again. As I sit there watching my mother working in the kitchen, I couldn't help but feel a little bit nervous. I have been thinking about "a match" all evening.

Yeah, I guess it's time. I finally come to a decision.

"Ma," I say, taking a deep breath. "I know that you mean well, and I appreciate your efforts to find me a wife. But I want to find love on my own terms," I begin.

"I understand!" Ma says, but she really doesn't. She has no idea what I am talking about.

"So… I mean… Would you mind sharing the credentials to the matrimony site so I can see the girl's profile for myself?" I ask hesitantly.

To my expectations, Ma looks a little bit taken aback, but she nods.

"Of course, beta. I understand. I just want you to be happy, and I know that you're capable of making your own decisions. The id is…" and then she gives me her email id and her password.

The password is a combination of my name and my date of birth. It isn't the strongest password, but it is the sweetest.

I write down the login information on a piece of paper and Ravi feel a sense of relief wash over me. It is my chance to take control of my love life and find someone who truly understands and appreciates me.

As I log into the site and begin to browse through the site, I can't help but feel a little bit excited. I kinda know that I am on the right path, and I can't wait to see what the future holds for me on this matrimony site.

As I scroll through my own profile phone, I can't believe what I am seeing. There, in black and white, is my profile on a popular matrimony app. And to make matters worse, my mother had been the one to register me.

Alright, I should get over it. What has been done is done. There is no point in sulking over it. It's time to see who the match is.

There are several matches. I click on one, and incidentally, this is the picture Ma had sent me.

Now, looking at the picture, she looks familiar. And so is her name.

I read through a profile and instantly know why she looks familiar.

Wait… She's my classmate Inara.

What are the odds?

Alright, so today is the day that I get 31 matches u

And, today is the day I find out that my mother has registered my profile on a matrimony app and is finding potential wife for me.

And, today is the day I match with my old crush's profile on a matrimony app.

Could life be more interesting?

There is a message from Inara, too. I eagerly click on it and read through it.

Hi Abhimanyu Singh,

It's Inara. I know it's been a while, but I thought I'd reach out. How have you been?"

Regards,

Inara

I hesitate for several minutes, my heart beating faster with every passing second. I am not sure what I am expecting, but I am hopeful. Maybe this time things would turn out differently.

I grin widely.

I have always had a bit of a crush on Inara. She was a shy girl and kept to herself during the college, so I could never ask her out.

But now, I can. I am thrilled to have the opportunity to finally ask her out. I quickly type out a message, asking her if she wants to grab a cup of coffee sometime.

To my delight, Inara replies almost immediately, saying that she would love to meet up with me.

We make plans for the coming weekend before signing out. I can't wait to finally see Inara again and explore the feelings that I have always had for her.

Chapter 3 – The date, awkward!

(Inara's POV)

I'm meeting Abhimanyu today, finally… After all these years, I have been nursing the grudges against him. But chatting with him, I realize that he might not be as bad as I think.

I'm ready with the outfit. A little black dress because it can never go wrong, pearls, bracelets and stilettoes.

Inara dear, are you ready for tonight?

I roll my eyes.

Correction—he is exactly the guy I think. He is just a prankster who would never stop teasing me.

We are meeting for coffee this evening. Why does he say as of we are hooking up tonight? He has a way to make things dirty. I cannot believe how tacky he is. Have all of my choices led to him or is he just that kind of guy?

Yeah.

I type a single word. I won't argue, that's what he wants.

Just remember, this isn't two classmates catching up. It's a date.

Seriously, what is up with him?

What does be mean by that?

Am I stupid?

I can almost picture his handsome face smirking with this message.

I am going to ignore his comment and reply with a simple 'Ok'.

Fuming over his words, I head to the cupboard and pull out something else.

I will get ready for the *date* alright!

✱✱✱

White shirt with folded sleeves, blue jeans, sneakers and my watch—this is my office look, the look that makes me look like an intimidating person.

I am pleasantly surprised as I arrive at the venue. It isn't a shady place as I had expected. It is a nice place, like a proper date place.

The cafe is a bright and airy space, with large windows letting in streams of sunlight. The walls are painted a cheerful pink and fuchsia and the furnishings are a mix of wooden tables and chairs and comfortable sofas. There are plants scattered throughout the cafe, giving it a fresh and vibrant feel.

The counter is bustling with activity as baristas take orders and prepare drinks. The smell of coffee and baked goods fills the air, making the cafe a popular spot for a mid-afternoon pick-me-up. There are a variety of pastries and sandwiches on display, and the glass case is filled with an assortment of muffins, scones, and croissants.

Customers of all ages are scattered throughout the cafe, chatting and laughing as they enjoy their drinks and snacks. Some are working on laptops, taking advantage of the cafe's free wifi, while others are catching up with friends over a cup of coffee. The atmosphere is lively and relaxed, with a friendly and welcoming vibe.

This is quiet cool. Even if the date doesn't go well, at least the ambience and the lively atmosphere will make my day.

A waiteress comes by two minutes after I sit down. I think this is a decent amount of time one needs to settle in before ordering anything. She hands me the menu with a polite smile.

"Regular water or bottled water, ma'am?" she asks.

"A latte with cheese sandwich, please!" I say.

I am pretty sure that Abhimanyu will be late, and the delicious aroma that wafts in my surrounding is just too delicious. When

I am already waiting for him when I see him coming through the glass door.

He is dressed in a crisp white shirt tucked neatly into his jeans with the sleeves folded to show his forearms which to my surprise I find quite drawn to; the way some boys try to dress, but fail miserably but Abhimanyu has aced that look. He walks into the café with the confidence of a man who knows he has made a good impression.

I gawk at him in awe. He spots me from a distance and smiles. He doesn't look disappointed as if he was expecting this. His gaze lingers down my neck and I curse under my breath. I may have left the button undone. Now, the shirt shows my clavicles and shows a V shape that ends just before my cleavage. I look down. That's far too much skin than I care to show.

Even my red mole is showing and that is sacred, something I have been saving only for "the one".

I have forgotten to button up properly and I don't have my stole, the one that I generally wrap in the office. This isn't going well. Now, if I button it, Abhimanyu would notice, and he would make fun of me.

Oh, the horror!

I feel the same horror I felt the day Abhimanyu Singh played that god awful prank of pitting us as the best couple. My face starts to burn.

Oh, the horror!

I look down again at my shirt and curse under my breath. I had been so nervous about her date with Abhimanyu that I completely forgotten to check my appearance before leaving the house.

And while I am still contemplating whether I should fix the faux paus, Abhimanyu reaches my table.

"Hi!" he flashes the brightest smile I have ever seen.

"Hi…" I smile shyly and wave at him. He takes a scene opposite me.

Now, as I sit across from Abhimanyu at the fancy restaurant, I couldn't help but feel a little embarrassed. I may have my apprehensions about a date with my nemesic, but I was still hoping to make a good impression. Now, all I can think of is that I am showing more skin than I care of, and that Abhimanyu might think I am trying to lead him on.

"Is everything okay?" Abhimanyu asks, eyeing me curiously. "You seem a little flustered."

So, he noticed that!

I blush.

"I'm so sorry, I can't believe I forgot to button up my shirt. I hope you don't think I'm trying to be inappropriate or anything."

His gaze lowers to look at my chest, only for a brief moment and then he quickly looks into my eyes.

Wow! Isn't he the gentleman? He surprises me.

"Ummm… You can button it up," he says softly.

His words surprises me even more.

And then, he picks up the menu and pretends to be perusing through it to find something good to order.

His action shocks the hell out of me. Abhimanyu doesn't seem like the same guy that I hated with all my might for almost five years. Since when did he become to considerate and such a thoroughly chivalrous man?

I quickly close the top two buttons.

There!

All better!

I clear my throat to get his attention, to tell him that I was all decent, to indicate that he can look at me...

But mostly, to get his attention...

Abhimanyu looks up at me and smiles, the smile that makes my heart flutter in my chest.

"Don't worry about it. It's just a shirt, and I didn't get any wrong idea," he says.

I smile back. I am not sure if we could date, but we could at least bury the animosity.

I mean, I can bury the animosity. He probably doesn't even remember what he had done to scar me for life.

The waitress brings my order and places it on the table.

"Welcome, sir! Are you ready to order now or should I come back in a few minutes?" she asks politely.

"I will have the same," Abhimanyu says with a polite smile. I can almost sense as if he wants the waitress to go away so he could focus on me. It could be just my imagination, but the feeling is quite strong.

"I thought this was a date," he says. He stretches his legs out and raises an eyebrow at me. His voice is rich and charming. My stomach flips at the sound of his voice.

"This *is* a date," I say. I guess?

"Then why did you order even before I came here?" he asks with a pout like a kid whose favourtie toy has been used without his permission, whose gift has been unwrapped in his absence.

"Ummm…" I don't know how to respond to that.

"So, you and I matching on a matrimony site, pretty crazy, huh?" he asks.

My thoughts, exactly. This is crazy.

"I never imagined to match with my nemesis," I say.

Abhimanyu looks shocked, which comes as a surprise to me. Surely he knows that I hated him.

I hate him, I still hate him, irrespective of how delicious he looks.

"What are you talking about?" he asks. "I am not your nemesis."

I stare at him. This was always understood – we were enemies. Why would he be surprised that I hate him? Doesn't he remember what he did to me during college fest?

"Yes, you are. I hated you ever since that incident…" My voice trails. I can't bring myself to talk about it. "Did you forget *that*?"

"Forget what?" Abhimanyu scratches his head, completely clueless. He looks so cute when he does that. Seriously, what's happening to me? I'm supposed to hate him. And what's wrong with him? he's supposed to remember about that incident.

"You know what I'm talking about," I say, exasperated.

"Nope, sorry," he says, still rubbing his head. "I have no idea."

I take a deep breath and try to calm down. This is not going the way I planned at all. I wanted to clear the air about that incident and then we could catch up just like two old classmates do and that would be about it.

But right now I'm stuck in the first step itself, because that handsome man with a devilish grin doesn't remember anything.

"You're telling me you don't know what happened in the final year of college?" I ask again.

"Nope." He says and he seems honest, but I can't say for sure. Maybe he's a terrific actor.

"And you don't know why I'm mad at you?" I ask. Right now, I feel like a fool. I recall that incident as if it happened yesterday and Abhimanyu has no clue. Was I wrong in harbouring such hatred all these years.

"I didn't know you are mad at me, and I have no idea why you would be mad at me."

"That's ridiculous!" I say. "You must remember something."

"No… I don't."

I can feel the frustration rising inside me.

"Are you sure?" I ask. "Maybe you just don't remember it because you dont want to remember."

Abhimanyu again rubs his head, this time a little faster. "I can assure you that I don't remember anything that I had done to upset you," he says.

I look at him and try to decide if he is telling the truth or just stringing me along.

"Okay," I say. "You turned me into a joke throughout the final year of engineering," I frown.

"What did I do?" he asks earnestly.

His eyes look distant and I just know what he is doing—he is trying to relive the past.

Abhimanyu's POV

I lean against the wall, trying to blend into the background as I listen to my seniors chatting. They're huddled in a group, laughing and chatting, and I can't help but overhear their conversation.

"I bet it's going to be Komal and me," Chetan says. "We're always so lovey-dovey, people love that."

"Nah, I don't think so," Arafat replies. "I think it's going to be Me and Naheed. We are discreet. Nobody likes public display of affection," he adds.

"That's right," Jai says. "Chetan and Komal are always holding hands and stealing kisses. It gets to my nerves at times."

"So what?" Chetan demands.

Jai ignores him.

"I think it will be Vivek and Anya... They are very sweet and they have a lot of friends even in juniors, so they might get more votes."

I roll my eyes, feeling a little bit annoyed. I hate the way they talk about love and relationships like it's some kind of game or competition. And I especially hate the way they assume that they're the ones who are going to win.

I decide to make my move.

"Hey, guys," I say, walking up to them with a confident smile. "I don't mean to intrude, but I couldn't help but overhear your conversation. And I have to say, I don't think any of you are going to win the 'best couple' award."

They all look at me, surprised.

"Oh yeah?" one of them says, raising an eyebrow. "And who do you think is going to win?"

I grin.

"Me and Inara. We're the ones who are truly in love, not just playing some kind of game. And I'm willing to bet on it."

They all laugh, shaking their heads.

"Dude, you aren't even together," Chetan says.

"Who say we aren't?? I ask him.

"You're on," Chetan says. "But be prepared to pay up if you lose."

Jai, the emcee steps up onto the platform, holding a microphone.

"Here we are again at the closing ceremony of department festival of the year. This year has been a little low-key, but we've seen some very nice ceremonies. Now, to announce the winner of the best couple award... Let's hear the nominees..."

He looks down at the cue card in his hand.

"Chetan and Komal..." the announcement is met with a cheer.

Chetan who has been anxiously sitting on their couch stands up in anticipation, and I nudge Komal who is blushing in response. Chetan grins like a proud father as he and Komal walk up to the stage. We crowd applaud and cheer with pride as the announcement is met with cheers and whistles.

"Arafat and Naheed," Jai calls.

This couple is welcomed with moderate excitement. Perhaps, it is only a few people who favour the couple. Arafat and Naheed get up at once, smiling as they walk to the stage, surrounded by cheers. The crowd applauds enthusiastically with pride, but their cheer does not quite match that of the first couple.

"Vivek and Anya..."

This couple is greeted with a roar of approval. Vivek and Anya are on their feet, jumping up and down and clapping in anticipation of the announcement. Vivek jumps in surprise when he hears his name called out. I guess he has not been expecting any sort of acknowledgement... perhaps even a grimace, but never applause. Anya nudges him hard in the arm, they walk up to the dais and take their place on the platform.

"I think the winner is clear," I whisper to myself because I have voted for the winners. I know the last couple will win.

Jai has one more couple to announce because he is looking down at the cue card. He looks straight at me with a strange look in his eye.

He waits for a moment, clears his throat, and moves on to the next introduction.

"Abhimanyu and Inara..."

There it is!

"Woohoo!" This meets with the loudest cheer of tonight. People are clapping frantically.

Inara turns to look at me with disbelief. It is My eyes meet with Inara's. I flash a smile.

I am so genuinely. I can feel the attention of everyone turning to us with interest. I notice Inara's face turning red. Oh, she's blusing.

My heart is thudding crazily as I get up and walk to Inara. With every step of mine, my heartbeat gets wilder and wilder.

I grin widely as I reach Inara and extends my hand. Everyone watches us expectantly. Following the pin-drop silence, Inara gets up, picks up her purse and leaves.

Are you effing kidding me?

I am going to lose my bet now.

Chapter 4 – The Revelation (Inara's POV)

I sit there watching Abhimanyu's face changing colours, and I know that he has recalled everything.

"I am sorry, inara. I had no idea that my silly behaviour during college days hurt you so much," he says with so much sincerity, i can't even be mad at him.

It feel's good that Abhimanyu is apologizing for his past behavior. It shows that he is mature and willing to take responsibility for his actions. I appreciate the apology and the effort to make amends... I can't stop but think that the two of Us may be able to move past the incident and continue our conversation or interaction without any lingering negative feelings.

Neither of us have spoken for a while.

"I'm really sorry about that prank I pulled on you in college," Abhimanyu says, looking at me with sincerity in his eyes. "It was stupid and immature, and I understand if you're still upset about it."

Alright, i admit. I was upset And offended by the prank, and i wanted to tell Abhimanyu abiut my r feelings and make him to understand my perspective. But then... He Has already d twice and reassured her that he is truly sorry for any harm that he may have caused. It might also be a good For him to ask me how he can make things right and demonstrate that he is committed to being a better person moving forward but then... I have nursed this grudge for five years. I want to let it go. I will forgive him and we will begin to like each otherm wouldn't that be something?.

"Hey, I'm sorry." Abhimanyu reaches out for my hand. "I was young and naive. I thought that a simple trick won't do any harm. If I knew that it would ruin my chances with you, I wouldn't have imagined doing anything like that."

Well... If he puts it like that, I can't fight with him, can I?

I smile softly and shake my head. "I appreciate your apology, Abhimanyu. It takes a lot of courage to admit when you're wrong. I've moved on from that incident and I'm willing to let it go."

Abhimanyu let's out a sigh of relief. "Thank you, Inara. I am glad that we reconnected after all these years. I don't want anything from the past to ruin it."

"Me neither," I say, taking a sip of my coffee.

We sit quietly for a while.

"I can't believe you didn't enjoy all the attention that night?" Abhimanyu looks genuinely surprised. "It was great fun!"

"It wasn't funny." I grit my teeth.

"It was. It was the best thing that happened in the final year." He is still in splits, and I want to wipe that smirk off his handsome face. I hate myself for loving his smile. I'm supposed to hate him. Why am I falling for his charm all over again?

"For you maybe..."

"Did you know I had to pay up because I had bet some guys about the same," he says.

The smile disappears from my face. Say what now? Wss that prank and that humiliation only for a bet?

Abhimanyu quickly realizes my changed mood.

Hey, they were betting who will win and i wanted to prove them wrong because love is not a competition. I had convinced nost of the computer science student, from all years, to vote for us. That's why they had cheered for us the loudest but since tou walked out, I lost to the couple who had the second highest votes, Vivek and Anya." Abhimanyu explains without even a pause to breath allmost ad if he fears I would leave it he doesn't tell me the truth.

And the truth has convinced me that he isn't the bad guy. I relax my shoulders and smile.

"may i suggest that we don't talk about our college days now? I say.

Abhimanyu nods vehemently.

"It's been great catching up with you. It's like no time has passed at all," i say. I am talking as if we were good friends in college, we weren't. But this is just polite conversation

Abhimanyu smiles.

"I feel the same way. You know, I've been thinking... I've always had a bit of a crush on you. I know it's probably unexpected and maybe even a little weird given our history, but I just had to tell you."

My eyes widened in surprise.

"Really? I had no idea."

Abhimanyu nods.

"I always thought you were smart, kind, and beautiful. I just never had the courage to tell you before. I hope it's not too late."

I hesitate for a moment before speaking.

"I have to admit, I've always had a bit of a crush on you too, Abhimanyu. I think we have a lot in common and I really enjoy spending time with you."

Abhimanyu's face brightens up with a huge grin.

"That's great to hear, Inara. I'm so glad we were able to reconnect and that there might be a chance for something more between us."

I smile back at him.

"Me too, Abhimanyu. I think we could be really good together."

As we finish our coffee and order another , I couldn't help but feel excited about the potential for a new relationship. Now that the past is behind us, I'm ready to move forward with open hearts and a fresh start.

We continue to chat, I couldn't help but feel grateful to have such a kind and understanding guy. I kinda have this feeling that they we are meant to be together but... That's crazy right? I have hated this guy for almost five years and now I can't wait to see what the future holds for us.

I am crazy!

Abhimanyu and I are deep in conversation, laughing and enjoying each other's company, when the cafe owner interrupts us. She was a tall, striking woman with long brown hair and a flirtatious smile.

"Hello there," she says leaning over the table and giving Abhimanyu a seductive look. "I couldn't help but notice how handsome you are. Would you like to join me for a drink later tonight?" she flashes a smile at Abhimanyu.

Then, she looks at me as if noticing my presence for the first time. She looks at me and nods curtly. "I'm Sasha, the owner of this cafe," she tells in a business tone before returning her attention to Abhimanyu.

Aha, so miss owner has a crush on Abhimanyu and doesn't mind interrupting the date.

"How is everything?" she asks.

My heart sinks. I have never the jealous kind, and I shouldn't even feel jealous of other women because I am here to see an old college friend; i am not on a date.

And yet, and I couldn't help but feel a twinge of insecurity at the cafe owner's bold advances. I know that I have no right to be jealous, but she couldn't shake the feeling that I am losing Abhimanyu's attention.

Abhimanyu, however, is unfazed by the Sasha's flirtatious behavior. He smiles politely.

"I'm sorry, but I'm here with my girlfriend. Maybe another time."

"It was nice," Abhimanyu says politely.

"Do you need anything else?" she fluttered her eyes rapidly.

Yeah, she is seriously into Abhimanyu she might not hesitate pulling him away from the table and into her office.

"Actually, we were about to leave," Abhimanyu says. It disappoints me. We are only just getting started. And he wants to leave already. Does this mean he doesn't like his first date with me? Or is he not interested in me? We could at least talk as friends.

Disappointment!

Utter disappointment!

Sasha, on the other hand, is still not backing down. She pouts as if that would change Abhimanyu's mind.

"Well, if you change your mind, you know where to find me." She winks at Abhimanyu and sashays away, leaving me feeling a little bit relieved.

"I will get the heck and then we are leaving," Abhimanyu says with determination. I purse my lips but nod. I can't let him notice my disappointment of this abrupt end to a perfect date.

A date?

It isn't a date. This is just two college friends meeting for a coffee and some chat. That's all. I watch Abhimanyu call for check, and keep the cash on the table.

"Let's go!" Abhimanyu says. "We should go some place else where nobody can disturb us."

Oh, wait!

So, he doesn't mean to end *this*, he's just moving *this* to somewhere else, what *this* is.

Alex suggests that they go somewhere else where they are not disturbed. Sarah offers to go to her apartment.

Did Abhimanyu notice that I was feeling a little bit flustered after the Sasha's interruption? Did he suggest that we go to some other place just for me? Can he see that I am feeling a little bit insecure?

Taht's so sweet.

He doesn't want me to feel uncomfortable.

"Sure!" I say and get up. I pick up my purse. Abhimanyu reaches for my hand and laces his fingers with mine.

"We can go for a walk or grab a drink somewhere a little bit quieter. I don't want you to feel like we're being disturbed."

I smile gratefully.

"That sounds like a great idea. But actually, I was thinking that maybe we could go back to my apartment. It's a little bit small, but it's cozy and we'll have some privacy."

Abhimanyu's eyes light up.

"I love that idea. Let's go."

As we make our way to my apartment, I couldn't help but feel a little bit giddy. Now, I realize that we have always been attracted to each other, and we wasted all those years in our silliness. Now, we both know that this is our chance to be alone and really explore their feelings.

Chapter 5 – The L-word
(Inara's POV)

I give Abhimanyu my address before driving home. Abhimanyu arrives a few minutes later. He is holding a bunch of colourful carnations for me, and I'm sure that's the reason for being late.

I don't mind one bit.

We sit on the couch and resume our conversation. I couldn't help but feel grateful to have such a loyal and considerate partner. I know that I have nothing to worry about with Abhimanyu by my side, and I couldn't wait to see what the future holds for us.

As we settle onto the couch and snuggle up together, we both sort of know that we have finally found what we have been looking for. We are not in love, but it wouldn't be long before we fall in love.

Abhimanyu laces his fingers with mine, and I let him. I can't think of anything except us—Abhimanyu and me. I can't think of anything else, not when my brain is asking me to just jump at him and kiss him insanely.

"If you could go back in time and change things what would you do?" he asks in the softest voice possible. It tickles me, and I feel a tingling sensation on my skin. How could someone's voice have such a deep impact on me?

"Inara?" he calls my name, hoping to get my attention.

Wow! I have never loved my name so much.

"Yeah... sorry... what were you saying?" I ask.

"I asked if you could go back in time and do it all over again, would you do it or change something?" he asks. His thumb is stroking mine, and I don't mind.

"Nothing... I might want to pay more attention in the date warehousing class because I work with the analytics team now and their words just bounce off me," I say.

Abhimanyu chuckles. He leans in closer. When he speaks, his voice drops to a whisper.

"I would have let loose a little. You were too uptight," he says with a teasing smile.

Alright, that does it. I'm not even considering him now. He is too annoying.

We keep quiet for a few minutes. Abhimanyu's words have touched me immensely. I suddenly find him attractive, just like I did before. I feel drawn to him, just like I did before. I can't look away from his way, just like I did before. All it takes is a little act of kindness, and all your grudges are washed away.

Tch... Such is life.

"Oh, and there is one more thing..." I say, breaking the silence. "Today, when you came to the café, I shouldn't have started by telling you about my shirt's button..." I say. He chuckles.

"Yeah, you shouldn't have. Not looking at you was probably the most difficult thing I have ever done in my life," he says and winks.

I know he is kidding.

"Thank you for not making it a big deal," I say. "It was so silly to..."

"Inara, Please..." he interrupts me. "Don't fret about it. What's important is that we're here, spending time together."

I smile, relieved.

"Thank you, Abhimanyu. You're so understanding. I really appreciate it."

We are quiet again.

Never before has Abhimanyu seemed more handsome or desirable to me. I want to speak to him and smile at him and look into his eyes. He has done exactly what I needed him to do. He had washed away the grudges of my college life, and it took him only a few kind words. The universe works in mysterious ways.

"What about you?" I finally break the silence. "What would you do differently, if you had a chance?" I ask.

"I would have asked you out instead of doing silly pranks," he says earnestly. I drop the spoon. He is looking at me with deep, intense, longing eyes. Oh. my. god. I could drown in those eyes. Is he talking about the same pranks that I was thinking about? His eyes were intense as they searched my face. He was serious. Maybe love isn't as dead as we thought. The longing in his eyes makes me blush. I lower my gaze and bite my lips.

He chuckles.

"You still do that? You haven't changed much in these five years."

"I don't bite my lips," I say curtly.

And that's a blatant lie.

"Yeah, you do," Abhimanyu says so firmly as if he knows me better than I know myself. I can't help but ask.

"How do you know?"

"Because I spent the better part of the last two semesters watching you. Every time you would see me you would bite your lips. It made you so irresistible..." His voice trails. He doesn't look away from my lips. I enjoy the attention, but it also makes me feel a million things, and my heart is thudding violently, so this needs to stop now.

"Alright, stop," I whisper but I can't wipe the smile off my face.

"You are smiling again, that's all I wanted," he says.

"Thank you," I say softly. "I thought you were just teasing about the whole asking-out thing."

"I am," he says just as earnestly as he had been through the evening. I glare at him. We both burst out laughing. Our laughter fills the cafe like music. The tension dissipates.

I decide to play along.

"If you wanted to ask me out, why didn't you?" I ask.

"I am sorry. But I was too afraid of losing you if I asked you out. I don't regret a thing. Not one thing. I just want you to know that I am sorry for that little prank. I never stopped loving you."

Wait…

What?

Did he just say the L-word?

"You what?" I ask. He smiles sheepishly.

"I liked you a lot. Why else would I pull a prank like that? I wanted people to see us as a couple. I wanted us to be a couple. But..." he stops midway.

"I... I am sorry as well. I am sorry that I never gave us a chance after that little prank. I am sorry that scared you away. I am sorry that I was so scared. I really was scared. But I know that we can't change the past. I know that the best thing to do is to let it go. To let the past stay in the past. I am sorry. I am just being honest. I am sorry that you are here and I am sorry that it is too late. I am so sorry."

He smiles.

"It is not too late," he whispers and reaches for my hand. I smile back at myself.

"So, do you want to go out with me?" he asks.

I nod.

"Want to catch a movie?"

"Why? Do you think you can take advantage of the darkness and kiss me?"

He looks as if I have caught him red-handed.

"Yeah?"

It's my turn to be dumbfounded.

"Stop playing pranks," I whisper and look away.

"I'm not joking," he says sincerely.

We have both been in love with each other for so long. I want him to know how I feel. I want him to see that we could be good together. His eyes are narrow as if he is thinking about something, making a decision or something.

Then he finally speaks.

"Can I have your parents' address? I would want to send my parents to talk to them," he says.

"Yeah, of course! It is time to put our animosity behind us," I joke.

I am disappointed. Why couldn't he propose to me?

I nod though.

"Do you want some coffee?" I ask tentatively. I hope that he changes his mind and asks me first before his parents talk to me.

"Sure!" He agrees.

After coffee, I offer to show him around my apartment. He quietly follows me. And now, it's time to show him the bedroom. The moment we enter my bedroom, he pushes me to the wall and presses his lips to mine. It is slow and sweet. He pulls back and looks me in the eyes. Our eyes are locked. There is no fear of rejection or fear of loss. We are both willing to suffer for this kiss.

"I love you, Inara," he whispers, and then he kisses me again. I have no idea how long the kiss was but it is over way too soon.

He kisses me again and I can taste the need in his sweet lips. His kisses are soft and gentle now.

I break free of his kiss.

"Will you marry me?" he asks.

"No!" I say. His face drops. He looks dejected.

"Just kidding!" I giggle. "You are not the only prankster."

"Once a prankster always a prankster," he says and plants a kiss on the tip of my nose.

"We are a couple of pranksters," I say.

"So, do you want to be pranksters forever?"

"Yes!"

*** THE END ***

Thanks for reading, please let me know of your feedback on my Facebook page https://www.facebook.com/smbikanu or shoot an email on smbikanu@gmail.com

About S. M. Bikanu

I'm just another sweet romance writer on Amazon KDP, aspiring to share stories every month—from my heart to your Kindle.

Wanna get in touch? DM on my Facebook page: https://www.facebook.com/smbikanu

Or shoot an email on smbikanu@gmail.com